Contents

KT-441-721

The food machine

A long tube joins your mouth to your bottom. It is called your **digestive system**. Food goes in through your mouth. Your body takes in the parts of food it can use. The rest comes out the other end as poo.

Did you know?

Your digestive system can be noisy and smelly. It produces burps, farts, and other bad-smelling things!

Disgusting Body Facts

Sick and Poo

Angela Royston

Raintree

www.raintreepublishers.co.uk
Visit our website to find out
more information about
Raintree books.

To order:
☎ Phone 0845 6044371
🖷 Fax +44 (0) 1865 312263
🖳 Email myorders@raintreepublishers.co.uk

Customers from outside the UK please telephone +44 1865 312262

©Raintree is an imprint of Capstone Global Library
Limited, a company incorporated in England and Wales
having its registered office at 7 Pilgrim Street, London,
EC4V 6LB – Registered company number: 6695582

Text © Capstone Global Library Limited 2010
First published in hardback in 2010
First published in paperback in 2011
The moral rights of the proprietor have been asserted.

Edited by Nancy Dickmann, Sian Smith, and
  Rebecca Rissman
Designed by Joanna Hinton Malivoire
Original illustrations ©Capstone Global Library 2010
Original illustrations by Christian Slade
Picture research by Tracy Cummins and Tracey Engel
Originated by Capstone Global Library Ltd
Printed and bound in China by Leo Paper Products Ltd

ISBN 978 1 4062 1305 8 (hardback)
14 13 12 11 10
10 9 8 7 6 5 4 3 2 1

ISBN 978 1 4062 1311 9 (paperback)
14 13 12 11 10
10 9 8 7 6 5 4 3 2 1

British Library Cataloguing in Publication Data
Royston, Angela.
  Sick and poo. -- (Disgusting body facts)
  1. Vomiting--Juvenile literature. 2. Defecation-- Juvenile
literature. 3. Feces--Juvenile literature.
  I. Title II. Series
  612.3'2-dc22

Acknowledgements
We would like to thank the following for permission to
reproduce photographs:
Age fotostock p. **11 background** (©simple stock shots);
Alamy pp. **7** (©Photodisc/Nick Koudis), **15** (©Phototake
Inc./Carol Donner); Getty Images pp. **13**, **20** (©Visuals
Unlimited/Dr. David Phillips), **23** (©Stone/TSI Pictures);
Photo Researchers, Inc. p. **25** (©Eye of Science);
Photolibrary p. **29** (©Steve Wisbauer); Shutterstock
pp. **11 bottom** (©Monkey Business Images), **11 middle**
(©RJ Lerich), **11 top** (©Emin Ozkan), **17 bottom**
(©Tischenko Irina), **17 top** (©Marie C. Fields), **19
bottom** (©ronfromyork), **19 middle**, **19 top** (©Marie
C. Fields), **27** (©Andrey Kudinov); Visuals Unlimited, Inc.
p. **9** (©Nucleus Medical Art).

Cover photograph reproduced with permission of Alamy
(©Poligons Photo Index).

Some words are shown in bold, **like this**. You can find
out what they mean by looking in the glossary.

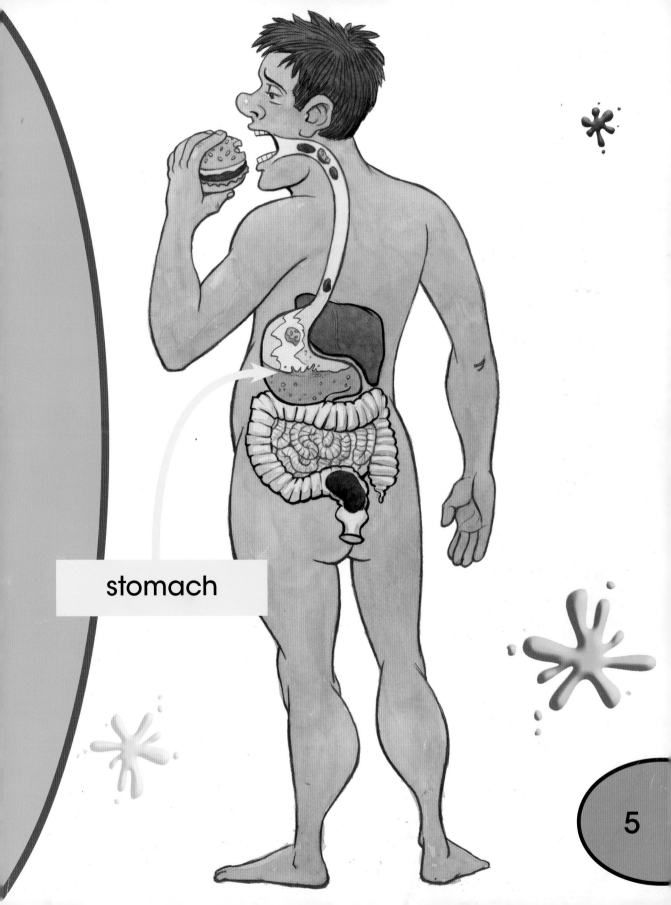

stomach

5

Sick

Sick is food that your stomach does not like! This is food you have already chewed up and swallowed. Unless you are sick, food stays in your stomach for about three hours.

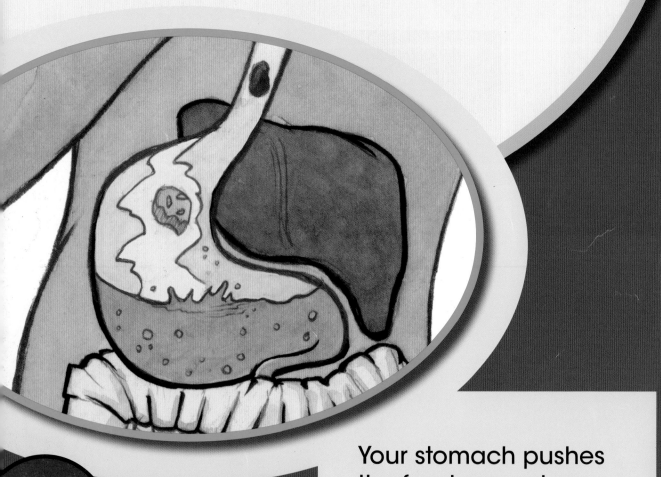

Your stomach pushes the food around so that it mixes with your stomach juices.

sick

Did you know?

The proper name for sick is "**vomit**". If you want to use an impressive word to describe being sick, say "**regurgitate**". It means to bring food back up again.

What happens when you are sick?

Your **oesophagus** [say "esofagus"] is the tube which joins your mouth to your stomach. Usually, a kind of gate called a **valve** stops food from moving back up this tube.

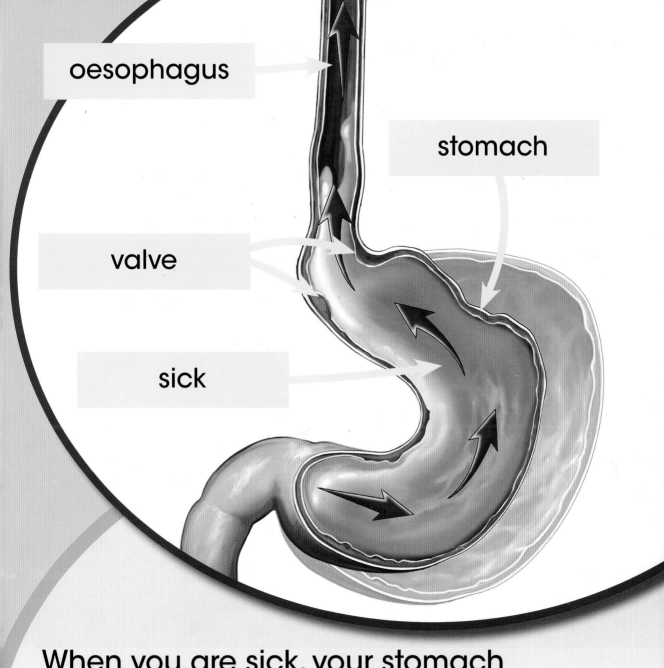

oesophagus

stomach

valve

sick

When you are sick, your stomach muscles squeeze your stomach. They force the sick through the valve. The sick goes back up your oesophagus and into your mouth.

9

What makes you sick?

Different things can make you sick.
They include:

- food that has gone bad
- food that was not properly cooked
- tiny living things called **germs**
- eating too much, too fast
- eating something very sweet and fatty
- the smell of someone else's sick!

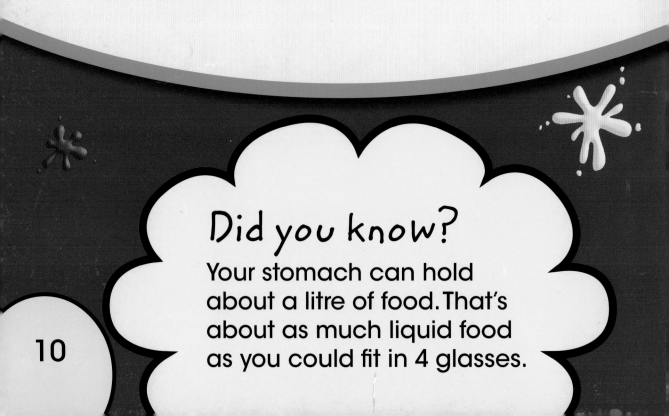

Did you know?

Your stomach can hold about a litre of food. That's about as much liquid food as you could fit in 4 glasses.

rotting tomatoes

rich, sweet chocolate cake

under-cooked meat

Why does sick smell?

Sick smells sour because it contains a liquid called **acid**. The acid is made by your stomach. The acid kills **germs** in your food. It also breaks down the food into smaller pieces.

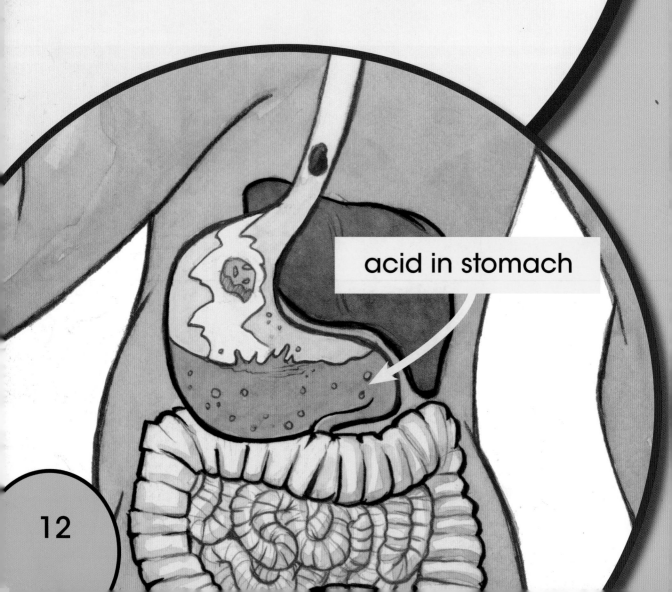

acid in stomach

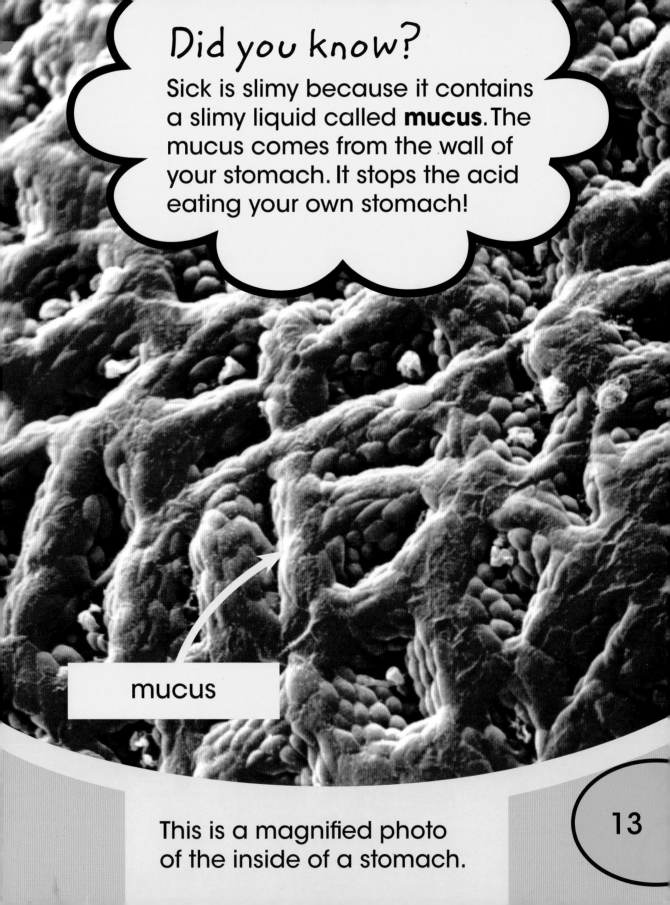

Did you know?

Sick is slimy because it contains a slimy liquid called **mucus**. The mucus comes from the wall of your stomach. It stops the acid eating your own stomach!

mucus

This is a magnified photo of the inside of a stomach.

Burping

Sometimes your stomach gets too much gas in it. Then the **valve** between the stomach and the **oesophagus** opens a little. The gas escapes up the tube from your stomach and out of your mouth. This is called burping!

gas

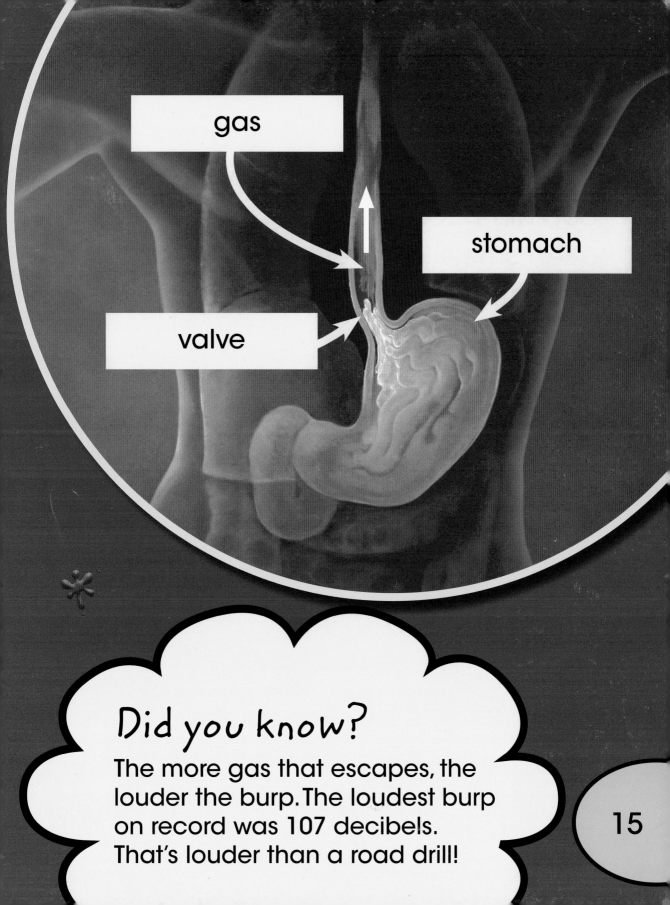

gas

stomach

valve

Did you know?

The more gas that escapes, the louder the burp. The loudest burp on record was 107 decibels. That's louder than a road drill!

What causes burps?

You burp when you swallow too much air or other gas. Fizzy drinks contain bubbles of gas. A burp often smells and tastes of the food or drink you have swallowed.

Did you know?

These are some of the things that can make you burp:
- fizzy drinks
- raw onion
- spicy food.

raw onion

fizzy drink

Poo

Most of your food is broken down so small it passes into your blood. **Fibre** is the parts of the food that cannot be broken down. It becomes part of your poo.

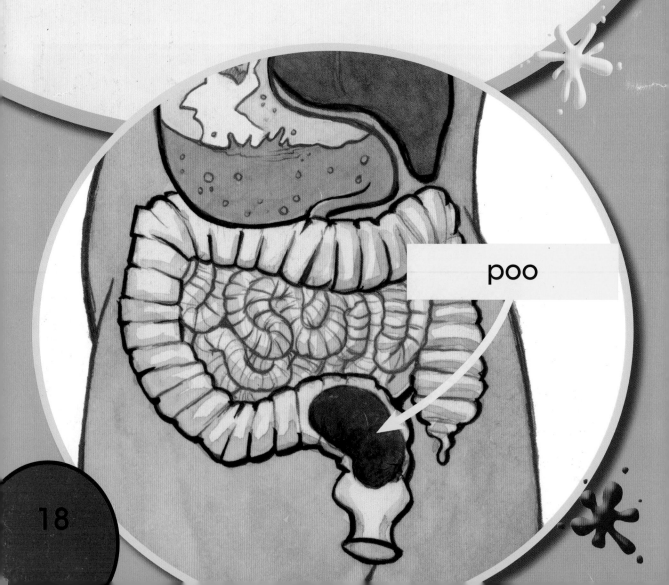

poo

18

These foods contain lots of fibre.

Did you know?

Fibre makes your poo bigger and softer, so it is easier to push out of your body.

What are farts?

Poo contains a type of **germ** called **bacteria**. The bacteria produce smelly gases. Sometimes they make too much gas. The extra gas escapes as a fart.

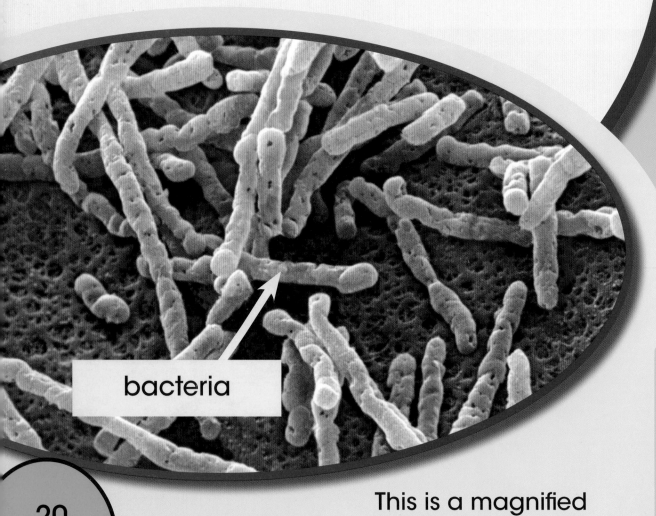

bacteria

This is a magnified photo of bacteria.

Did you know?

Everyone farts several times a day, but some farts smell more than others. The biggest farts make the most noise!

21

Getting rid of poo

Poo moves along a wide tube in your body called the **large intestine**. It slowly piles up at the end of the tube. You push poo out of your body through a hole called the **anus**.

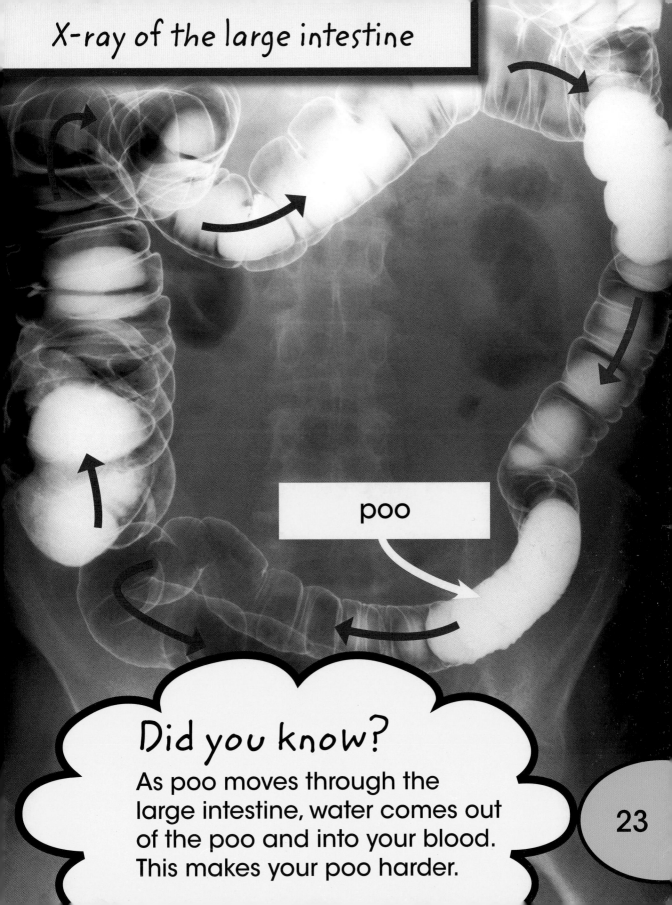

poo

Did you know?

As poo moves through the large intestine, water comes out of the poo and into your blood. This makes your poo harder.

23

Diarrhoea

You get diarrhoea when your poo contains too much water. This happens when the poo moves through your **large intestine** too quickly. There is not enough time for the water to move into your blood.

germ that
causes dysentery

Germs can cause
diarrhoea. Dysentery is a
type of diarrhoea that is
so bad it can kill you.

Constipation

Sometimes your poo contains too little water. The poo becomes so hard it is difficult to push it out of your body. This is called **constipation**. It can be very painful.

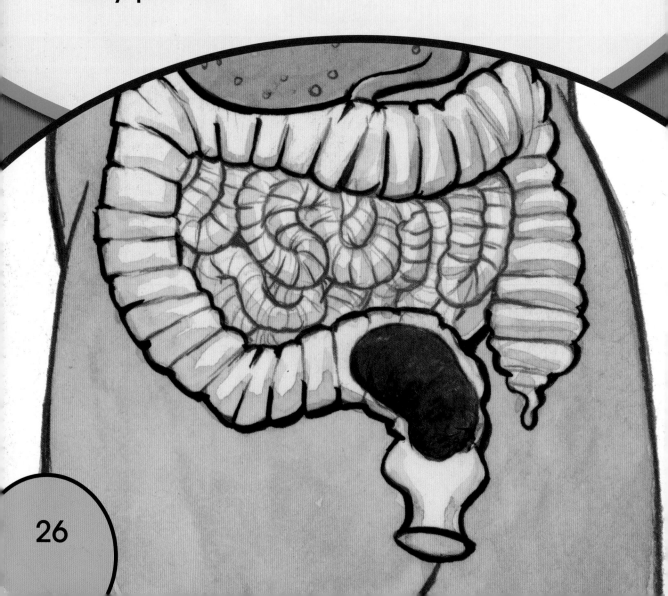

Did you know?
Camels have incredibly dry poo. This helps them to save water in the desert.

camel poo

More about the digestive system

If your **digestive system** was spread out it would be about 5–6 times as long as your body.

About three-quarters of your poo is water.

You often get lots of liquid called **saliva** in your mouth just before you are sick. **Acid** in sick can damage your teeth and this saliva helps to protect them.

Poo is brown because it contains bile. Bile breaks up fat in your food. It is yellow or green. Bile mixes with poo and stains it brown.

Even if you didn't eat, you would still make poo. Poo contains **mucus**, **bacteria**, and dead skin.

Glossary

acid sour liquid that breaks down food and other solids

anus opening in your bottom at the end of the digestive system

bacteria tiny living things. Bacteria are a type of germ.

constipation when poo is so hard it is difficult to push out of the body

digestive system the parts of the body that deal with the food you eat

fibre parts of food that the body cannot break down

germs tiny living things that can make you ill if they get inside your body

large intestine wide tube that takes waste food to the anus

mucus slimy liquid found inside the body

oesophagus tube that joins the mouth and throat to the stomach

regurgitate to vomit or be sick

saliva liquid in the mouth. Saliva is also called "spit".

valve part of the body that works like a gate

vomit food brought back up from the stomach through the mouth. Vomit is also called "sick".

Find out more

Find out

Why does some poo float?

Books

My Amazing Body: Eating,
Angela Royston (Raintree, 2004)

My Best Book of the Human Body, Barbara Taylor
(Kingfisher Books, 2008)

Up Close Human Body, Paul Harrison
(Franklin Watts, 2009)

Websites

**kids.aol.co.uk/stinky-stinky-poo-facts/
article/20080613061809990001**
This fun website is full of interesting facts about
poo. Click on the "Sick vomitous facts" link for
interesting facts about vomit.

**www.childrenfirst.nhs.uk/juniors/fun/germzap.
html**
This website has an animation of how germs
can cause vomiting.

www.hygiene-educ.com/en/home.htm
Fun website with games and information about
germs and how to avoid them.

Index